Faith

Promises to Inspire Your Heart

Pi Pocket
INSPIRATIONS

summerside
PRESS

Contents

I Believe

Faith allows us to continually delight in life
since we have placed our needs in God's hands.

JANET WEAVER SMITH

I believe in the sun even if it isn't shining.
I believe in love even when I am alone.
I believe in God even when He is silent.

Faith is not shelter against difficulties,
but belief in the face of all contradictions.

PAUL TOURNIER

If it can be verified, we don't need faith....
Faith is for that which lies on the other side of reason.
Faith is what makes life bearable, with all its
tragedies and ambiguities and sudden, startling joys.

MADELEINE L'ENGLE

To believe in God starts with a conclusion about Him,
develops into confidence in Him, and then
matures into a conversation with Him.

STUART BRISCOE

Pure gold put in the fire comes out of it proved pure;
genuine faith put through this suffering comes out
proved genuine.... It's your faith, not your gold, that
God will have on display as evidence of his victory.

1 PETER 1:6–7 MSG

I am convinced beyond a shadow of any doubt
that the most valuable pursuit we can
embark upon is to know God.

KAY ARTHUR

*Faith is not belief without proof,
but trust without reservations.*

ELTON TRUEBLOOD

For Himself

Although it be good to think upon
the kindness of God, and to love Him and
worship Him for it; yet it is far better
to gaze upon the pure essence of Him and to
love Him and worship Him for Himself.

We desire many things,
and God offers us only one thing.
He can offer us only one thing—Himself.
He has nothing else to give.
There is nothing else to give.

PETER KREEFT

The reason for loving God is God Himself,
and the measure in which we should love Him
is to love Him without measure.

BERNARD OF CLAIRVAUX

There is an essential connection between
experiencing God, loving God, and trusting God.
You will trust God only as much as you love Him,
and you will love Him to the extent you have
touched Him, rather that He has touched you.

BRENNAN MANNING

You alone are the LORD.
You made the heavens...,
the earth and all that is on it,
the seas and all that is in them.
You give life to everything, and
the multitudes of heaven worship you.

NEHEMIAH 9:6 NIV

*It is in silence that God is known, and
through mysteries that He declares Himself.*

ROBERT H. BENSON

Faith Shines Through

As a countenance is made beautiful by
the soul's shining through it, so the world is
beautiful by the shining through it of God.

FREDRICH HEINRICH

*I see Heaven's glories shine,
and faith shines equal,
arming me from fear.*

EMILY BRONTË

Our feelings do not affect God's facts.
They may blow up, like clouds, and cover
the eternal things that we do most truly believe.
We may not see the shining of the promises—
but they still shine!

AMY CARMICHAEL

So keep a firm grip on the faith....
It won't be long before this generous God
who has great plans for us in Christ...will have you
put together and on your feet for good.

1 PETER 5:9–10 MSG

Begin today! No matter how feeble the light,
let it shine as best it may. The world may need
just that quality of light which you have.

HENRY C. BLINN

One taper lights a thousand,
Yet shines as it has shone;
And the humblest light may kindle
A brighter than its own.

HEZEKIAH BUTTERWORTH

You are a child of your heavenly Father.
Confide in Him. Your faith in His love and power
can never be bold enough.

BASILEA SCHLINK

This is my Father's world;
He shines in all that's fair.
In the rustling grass I hear Him pass;
He speaks to me everywhere.

MALTBIE D. BABCOCK

Providing All Our Needs

Each of us may be sure that if God sends us
on stony paths He will provide us with strong shoes,
and He will not send us out on any journey
for which He does not equip us well.

ALEXANDER MACLAREN

God provides resting places as well as
working places. Rest, then, and be thankful
when He brings you, wearied, to a wayside well.

L. B. COWMAN

Your ears shall hear a word behind you, saying,
"This is the way, walk in it," whenever you turn
to the right hand or whenever you turn to the left.

ISAIAH 30:21 NKJV

Where there is faith, there is love.
Where there is love, there is peace.
Where there is peace, there is God.
Where there is God, there is no need.

God cares for the world He created, from
the rising of a nation to the falling of the sparrow.
Everything in the world lies under the watchful
gaze of His providential eyes, from the numbering
of the days of our life to the numbering of the
hairs on our head. When we look at the world
from that perspective, it produces within us
a response of reverence.

KEN GIRE

If you have a special need today,
focus your full attention on the goodness
and greatness of your Father rather than
on the size of your need. Your need is
so small compared to His ability to meet it.

A new path lies before us;
we're not sure where it leads;
But God goes on before us,
providing all our needs.

LINDA MAURICE

Faith for the Future

God may be invisible, but He's in touch.
You may not be able to see Him, but He is in control.
And that includes you—your circumstances.
That includes what you've just lost.
That includes what you've just gained.
That includes all of life—past, present, future.

CHARLES SWINDOLL

Faith makes the uplook good,
the outlook bright, the inlook favorable,
and the future glorious.

V. RAMOND EDMAN

Joy comes from knowing God loves me
and knows who I am and where I'm going...
that my future is secure as I rest in Him.

JAMES DOBSON

Never be afraid to trust an unknown future
to an all-knowing God.

CORRIE TEN BOOM

No matter what our past may have held,
and no matter how many future days we have,
[God] stands beside us and loves us.

GARY SMALLEY AND JOHN TRENT

Great is the LORD and greatly to be praised; and His
greatness is unsearchable.... The LORD is good to all,
and His tender mercies are over all His works.

PSALM 145:3, 9 NKJV

How could I be anything but quite happy
if I believed always that all the past is forgiven,
and all the present furnished with power,
and all the future bright with hope.

JAMES SMETHAM

*I don't know what the future holds,
but I know who holds the future.*

E. STANLEY JONES

With Every Breath

God doesn't want us to just depend on Him as
a last resort.... He wants us to depend on Him
for every breath we take. And...that kind
of dependent life is not stifling. It's liberating!

STORMIE OMARTIAN

This is the real gift: we have been given
the breath of life, designed with a unique,
one-of-a-kind soul that exists forever—
whether we live it as a burden or a joy or with
indifference doesn't change the fact that we've
been given the gift of being now and forever.
Priceless in value, we are handcrafted by God,
who has a personal design and plan for each of us.

WENDY MOORE

We have come to know and have believed
the love which God has for us. God is love,
and the one who abides in love abides in God,
and God abides in him.

1 JOHN 4:16 NASB

There is nothing but God's grace. We walk upon it;
we breathe it; we live and die by it;
it makes the nails and axles of the universe.

ROBERT LOUIS STEVENSON

To be grateful is to recognize the Love of God
in everything He has given us—
and He has given us everything.
Every breath we draw is a gift of His love,
every moment of existence is a gift of grace.

THOMAS MERTON

On that day the LORD their God
will rescue his people,
just as a shepherd rescues his sheep.
They will sparkle in his land
like jewels in a crown.

ZECHARIAH 9:16 NLT

*God knows the rhythm of my spirit
and knows my heart thoughts.
He is as close as breathing.*

The Faith Within

No journey carries one far unless,
as it extends into the world around us,
it goes an equal distance into the world within.

LILLIAN SMITH

For the LORD searches every heart....
If you seek him, he will be found by you.

1 CHRONICLES 28:9 NIV

Within each of us there is an inner place
where the living God Himself longs to dwell,
our sacred center of belief.

Let us not set the standards of our conquest
to mean the maintenance of comfort but rather,
the development of an inner presence.

CHRISTOPHER DE VINCK

As you have received Christ Jesus the Lord,
so walk in Him, having been firmly rooted
and now being built up in Him and
established in your faith.

COLOSSIANS 2:6–7 NASB

The Lord's chief desire is to reveal Himself to you
and, in order for Him to do that, He gives you
abundant grace. The Lord gives you the experience
of enjoying His presence. He touches you,
and His touch is so delightful that, more than ever,
you are drawn inwardly to Him.

MADAME JEANNE GUYON

Our inner happiness depends not
on what we experience but on the degree of
our gratitude to God, whatever the experience.

ALBERT SCHWEITZER

Walk and talk and work and laugh with your friends,
but behind the scenes, keep up the life of
simple prayer and inward worship.

THOMAS R. KELLY

*God waits for us in the
inner sanctuary of the soul.
He welcomes us there.*

RICHARD J. FOSTER

Grow in Love

It is an extraordinary and beautiful thing
that God, in creation...works with the beauty
of matter; the reality of things; the discoveries of
the senses, all five of them; so that we, in turn,
may hear the grass growing; see a face
springing to life in love and laughter....
The offerings of creation...our glimpses of truth.

MADELEINE L'ENGLE

Love is a tender plant; when properly nourished,
It becomes sturdy and enduring.

H. B. BROWN

In the deepest heart of every human
God planted a longing for Himself,
as He is: a God of love.

EUGENIA PRICE

*I believe that life is given us
so we may grow in love.*

HELEN KELLER

God is the sunshine that warms us,
the rain that melts the frost and
waters the young plants.
The presence of God is a climate of
strong and bracing love, always there.

JOAN ARNOLD

Love allows us to live,
and through living we grow in loving.

EVELYN MANDEL

We ought always to thank God for you...
and rightly so, because your faith is growing
more and more, and the love every one of you
has for each other is increasing.

2 THESSALONIANS 1:3 NIV

Love is little deeds we show,
Love will make my spirit grow;
Grow in peace, grow in light
Love will do the thing that's right.

CHARLES DALMON

Through His Power

In difficulties, I can drink freely of God's power
and experience His touch of refreshment and blessing—
much like an invigorating early spring rain.

ANABEL GILLHAM

Should we feel at times disheartened and
discouraged, a simple movement of heart toward
God will renew our powers. Whatever He may
demand of us, He will give us at the moment
the strength and courage that we need.

FRANÇOIS FÉNELON

Look for the weak people in your life today,
and see if you can discover what makes them strong,
for then you will understand God's power.

CHRISTOPHER DE VINCK

Human love would never have the power it has
were it not rooted in an express image of God.

J. MOUROUX

·

This life is not all. It is an "unfinished symphony"...
with those who know that they are related to God
and have felt "the power of an endless life."

HENRY WARD BEECHER

O troubled heart, tho' thy foes unite,
let thy faith be strong and thy armor bright;
Thou shall overcome thro' His power and might,
and more than conqueror be.

FANNY CROSBY

In all these things we are more than conquerors
through him who loved us.

ROMANS 8:37 NIV

Prayer imparts the power to walk and not faint.

OSWALD CHAMBERS

In God's Hands

If we pray for anything according to the
will of God, we already have what we pray for
the moment we ask it. We do not know exactly
when it will arrive; but we...have learned to
leave this in His hands, and to live just as happily
whether the answer arrives immediately or later.

OLE HALLESBY

It is such a comfort to drop the tangles of life into
God's hands and leave them there.

L. B. COWMAN

God is able to make all grace abound to you,
so that in all things at all times, having all that
you need, you will abound in every good work.

2 CORINTHIANS 9:8 NIV

The devout soul is always safe in every state, if it makes everything an occasion either of rising up, or falling down into the hands of God, and exercising faith, and trust, and resignation to Him.

WILLIAM LAW

God writes with a pen that never blots, speaks with a tongue that never slips, and acts with a hand that never fails.

HUBERT VAN ZELLER

Nothing happens to us that God hasn't already handled before.

JANETTE OKE

Until we meet again, may God hold you in the palm of His hand.

Beyond Expectations

One of the most wonderful things about
knowing God is that there's always so much
more to know, so much more to discover.
Just when we least expect it, He intrudes
into our neat and tidy notions about
who He is and how He works.

JONI EARECKSON TADA

Keep close to your rule, the Word of God,
and to your guide, the Spirit of God,
and never be afraid of expecting too much.

JOHN WESLEY

I asked God for all things that I might enjoy life.
He gave me life that I might enjoy all things.

*Faith expects from God
what is beyond all expectations.*

What have we to expect? Anything.
What have we to hope for? Everything.
What have we to fear? Nothing.

EDWARD B. PUSEY

God wants us to approach life,
full of expectancy that God is going to
be at work in every situation as we
release our faith in Him.

COLIN URQUHART

You pay God a compliment
by asking great things of Him.

TERESA OF AVILA

Divine guidance is promised to us,
and our faith must therefore
confidently look for and expect it.

HANNAH WHITALL SMITH

Truly, O God of Israel, our Savior,
you work in mysterious ways.

ISAIAH 45:15 NLT

God Will Make a Way

Part of our job is simply to be...always attentive to
what we are doing and what is going on inside us,
at the same time we listen and pay attention
to the people and events around us. Part of our job
is to expect that, if we are attentive and willing,
God will "give us prayer," will give us the things
we need, "our daily bread," to heal and grow in love.

ROBERTA BONDI

If we just give God the little that we have,
we can trust Him to make it go around.

GLORIA GAITHER

Know that wisdom is such to your soul;
if you find it, you will find a future,
and your hope will not be cut off.

PROVERBS 24:14 NRSV

Peace *with* God brings the peace *of* God.
It is a peace that settles our nerves, fills our mind,
floods our spirit, and in the midst of the uproar
around us, gives us the assurance
that everything is all right.

BOB MUMFORD

None of us knows what the next change is going to be,
what unexpected opportunity is just around the corner,
waiting to change all the tenor of our lives.

KATHLEEN NORRIS

God is with us, and His power is around us.

CHARLES H. SPURGEON

And the peace of God, which transcends all
understanding, will guard your hearts
and your minds in Christ Jesus.

PHILIPPIANS 4:7 NIV

Always There

God has put into each of our lives a void
that cannot be filled by the world.
We may leave God or put Him on hold,
but He is always there, patiently waiting
for us...to turn back to Him.

EMILIE BARNES

And I am convinced that nothing can ever separate
us from God's love. Neither death nor life,
neither angels nor demons, neither our fears for today
nor our worries about tomorrow.

ROMANS 8:38 NLT

We are always in the presence of God....
There is never a nonsacred moment!
His presence never diminishes. Our awareness
of His presence may falter, but the reality
of His presence never changes.

MAX LUCADO

Eating lunch with a friend. Trying to do
a decent day's work. Hearing the rain patter
against the window. There is no event so
commonplace but that God is present within it,
always hiddenly, always leaving you room to
recognize Him or not to recognize Him,
but all the more fascinatingly because of that,
all the more compellingly and hauntingly.

FREDERICK BUECHNER

Fear not tomorrow, God is already there.

Even when we cannot see the why and
wherefore of God's dealings, we know that
there is love in and behind them,
and so we can rejoice always.

J. I. PACKER

*God's hand is always there; once you grasp it
you'll never want to let it go.*

Proven Promises

God has not promised skies always blue,
flower-strewn pathways all our lives through;
God has not promised sun without rain,
joy without sorrow, peace without pain.
But God has promised strength for the day,
rest for the labor, light for the way,
grace for the trials, help from above,
unfailing sympathy, undying love.

ANNIE JOHNSON FLINT

The Lord doesn't always remove the sources of stress
in our lives...but He's always there and cares for us.
We can feel His arms around us on the darkest night.

JAMES DOBSON

We may...depend upon God's promises,
for...He will be as good as His word.
He is so kind that He cannot deceive us,
so true that He cannot break His promise.

MATTHEW HENRY

All that we have and are is one of the unique
and never-to-be repeated ways God has chosen
to express Himself in space and time.
Each of us, made in His image and likeness,
is yet another promise He has made to the universe
that He will continue to love it and care for it.

BRENNAN MANNING

The hope we have in Christ is an absolute certainty.
We can be sure that the place Christ is preparing
for us will be ready when we arrive, because
with Him nothing is left to chance.
Everything He promised He will deliver.

BILLY GRAHAM

As for God, His way is perfect;
the word of the LORD is proven;
He is a shield to all who trust in Him.

2 SAMUEL 22:31 NKJV

Continual Delight

Do you know why the mighty God of the
universe chooses to answer prayer? It is because
His children ask. God delights in our asking.
He is pleased at our asking. His heart
is warmed by our asking.

RICHARD J. FOSTER

I will answer them before they even call to Me.
While they are still talking about their needs,
I will go ahead and answer their prayers!

ISAIAH 65:24 NLT

God loves us, not because we are lovable
but because He is love, not because
He needs to receive but because
He delights to give.

C. S. LEWIS

All [God's] glory and beauty come from within,
and there He delights to dwell. His visits
there are frequent, His conversation sweet,
His comforts refreshing, His peace
passing all understanding.

THOMAS À KEMPIS

Joy is perfect acquiesce in God's will
because the soul delights itself in God Himself.

H. W. WEBB-PEPLOE

We have a Father in heaven who is almighty, who
loves His children as He loves His only-begotten Son,
and whose very joy and delight it is to...help them
at all times and under all circumstances.

GEORGE MUELLER

*Faith allows us to continually delight in life
since we have placed our needs in God's hands.*

JANET L. WEAVER SMITH

Live Fully

Live fully each moment of today.
Trust God to let you work through it.
He will give you all you need.
Don't skip over the painful...moment—
even it has its important and rightful place.

You will find as you look back upon your life,
that the moments when you have really lived
are the moments when you have
done things in the spirit of love.

HENRY DRUMMOND

Live your life while you have it.
Life is a splendid gift—
there is nothing small about it.

FLORENCE NIGHTINGALE

Go after God, who piles on all the riches
we could ever manage.

1 TIMOTHY 6:17 MSG

Into all our lives, in many simple, familiar,
homely ways, God infuses this element of joy
from the surprises of life, which unexpectedly
brighten our days, and fill our eyes with light.

SAMUEL LONGFELLOW

Don't just get older, get better. Live realistically.
Give generously. Adapt willingly.
Trust fearlessly. Rejoice daily.

CHARLES SWINDOLL

Each day is a little life. Live it to its fullest.

Be such a person, and live such a life,
that if every one were such as you,
and every life a life such as yours,
this earth would be God's paradise.

PHILLIPS BROOKS

Praise Follows Trust

They that trust the Lord
find many things to praise Him for.
Praise follows trust.

LILY MAY GOULD

There is an activity of the spirit, silent, unseen,
which must be the dynamic of any form of truly
creative, fruitful trust. When we commit a
predicament, a possibility, a person to God in
genuine confidence, we do not merely step aside
and tap our foot until God comes through.
We remain involved. We remain in
contact with God in gratitude and praise.

EUGENIA PRICE

I will praise you forever, O God,
for what you have done.
I will trust in your good name
in the presence of your faithful people.

PSALM 52:9 NLT

God came to us because God wanted to join us
on the road, to listen to our story, and to help us
realize that we are not walking in circles but
moving toward the house of peace and joy....
The God of love who gave us life sent us [the] only
Son to be with us at all times and in all places,
so that we never have to feel lost in our struggles
but always can trust that God walks with us.

HENRI J. M. NOUWEN

Praise Him for all that is past.
Trust Him for all that is to come.

JOSEPH HART

Trust God where you cannot trace Him.
Do not try to penetrate the cloud He brings
over you; rather look to the bow that is on it.
The mystery is God's; the promise is yours.

JOHN MACDUFF

Believing and Doing

You can no more show me your works apart from
your faith than I can show you my faith apart
from my works. Faith and works, works and faith,
fit together hand in glove.

JAMES 2:18 MSG

Strive for excellence. Don't try to get by with less.
Don't slough off. Don't ignore your responsibilities.
One of the best ways to make your faith ring true...
is by your commitment to excellence and honesty.

KEN DAVIS

A Christian should always remember that the
value of his or her good works is not based on their
number and excellence, but on the love of God
which prompts one to do these things.

JUAN DE LA CRUZ

Work is my primary expression of faith
and praise to God, my service to the neighbors
He commands me to love, my responsible
stewardship of His gifts, and the most efficient
means of communicating the good news
of salvation to the world.

JUDITH ALLEN SHELLY

Great works do not always lie our way,
but every moment we may do little ones
excellently, that is, with great love.

FRANCIS DE SALES

All work that is worth anything is done in faith.

ALBERT SCHWEITZER

Eternity in Our Hearts

Let Jesus be in your heart,
Eternity in your spirit,
The world under your feet,
The will of God in your actions.
And let the love of God shine forth from you.

CATHERINE OF GENOA

We do not look at the things which are seen,
but at the things which are not seen.
For the things which are seen are temporary,
but the things which are not seen are eternal.

2 CORINTHIANS 4:18 NKJV

I thank You, O Lord, that You have so set
eternity within my heart that no earthly thing
can ever satisfy me wholly.

JOHN BAILLIE

Deep within us all there is an amazing inner sanctuary of the soul, a holy place...to which we may continuously return. Eternity is at our hearts, pressing upon our time-torn lives, warming us... calling us home unto Itself. Yielding to these persuasions...utterly and completely, to the Light within, is the beginning of true life.

THOMAS R. KELLY

Live near to God, and so all things will appear to you little in comparison with eternal realities.

ROBERT MURRAY M'CHEYNE

We have been in God's thought from all eternity, and in His creative love, His attention never leaves us.

MICHAEL QUOIST

The Light of Faith

Happy is the person who knows what to
remember of the past, what to enjoy in
the present, and what to plan for the future.

ARNOLD GLASOW

There is a past which is gone forever,
but there is a future which is still our own.

F. W. ROBERTSON

Trust the past to the mercy of God,
the present to His love, and
the future to His Providence.

AUGUSTINE

To believe in something not yet proved
and to underwrite it with our lives;
it is the only way we can leave the future open.

LILLIAN SMITH

You can never change the past. But by the grace of God, you can win the future. So remember those things which will help you forward, but forget those things which will only hold you back.

RICHARD C. WOODSOME

Forgetting what is behind and straining toward what is ahead, I press on toward the goal to win the prize for which God has called me heavenward.

PHILIPPIANS 3:13 NIV

The uncertainties of the present always give way to the enchanted possibilities of the future.

GELSEY KIRKLAND

Cease to inquire whatever the future has in store, and take as a gift whatever the day brings forth.

HORACE

The only light upon the future is faith.

THEODORE HOECKER

Tied to the Infinite

In comparison with this big world, the human heart
is only a small thing. Though the world is so large,
it is utterly unable to satisfy this tiny heart.
Our ever growing soul and its capacities can be
satisfied only in the infinite God. As water is
restless until it reaches its level, so the soul
has no peace until it rests in God.

SADHU SUNDAR SINGH

We need time to dream, time to remember,
and time to reach the infinite. Time to be.

GLADYS TABER

The Lord's loving kindnesses indeed never cease,
for His compassions never fail. They are new
every morning; great is Your faithfulness.

LAMENTATIONS 3:22–23 NASB

An infinite God can give all of Himself to each of His children. He does not distribute Himself that each may have a part, but to each one He gives all of Himself as fully as if there were no others.

A. W. Tozer

The Infinite has sowed His name in the heaven in burning stars, but on the earth He has sowed His name in tender flowers.

Jean Paul Richter

Faith is the subtle chain that binds us to the infinite.

Elizabeth Oakes Smith

You are in the Beloved...therefore infinitely dear to the Father, unspeakably precious to Him. You are never, not for one second, alone.

Norman Dowty

A Step of Faith

Great faith isn't the ability to believe
long and far into the misty future.
It's simply taking God at His word
and taking the next step.

JONI EARECKSON TADA

For the very structures of earth are God's;
He has laid out His operations on a firm foundation.
He protectively cares for His faithful friends,
step by step.

1 SAMUEL 2:8–9 MSG

*I would rather walk with God in the dark
than go alone in the light.*

MARY GARDINER BRAINARD

I said to the man who stood at the gate of the year,
I said to a man who stood at the gate of the year,
"Give me a light that I may tread safely into
the unknown." And he replied, "Go out into the
darkness and put your hand in the hand of God.
That shall be to you better than a light
and safer than a known way."

M. LOUISE HASKINS

Hope does not necessarily take the form of
excessive confidence; rather, it involves
the simple willingness to take the next step.

STANLEY HAUERWAS

When you come to the edge of all the light you
have, and must take a step into the darkness of the
unknown, believe that one of two things will happen.
Either there will be something solid for you to
stand on—or you will be taught how to fly.

PATRICK OVERTON

Belonging to Him

If we really fully belong to God, then we must
be at His disposal and we must trust in Him.
We must never be preoccupied with the future.
There is no reason to be. God is there.

MOTHER TERESA

Those who know God have great contentment in God.
There is no peace like the peace of those whose
minds are possessed with full assurance that they
have known God, and God has known them, and that
this relationship guarantees God's favor to them
in life, through death and on forever.

J. I. PACKER

I have held many things in my hands and I have
lost them all; but whatever I have placed
in God's hands, that I still possess.

MARTIN LUTHER

Peace of conscience, liberty of heart,
the sweetness of abandoning ourselves in the
hands of God, the joy of always seeing the light
grow in our hearts, finally, freedom from the fears
and insatiable desires of the times, multiply a
hundredfold the happiness which the true
children of God possess in the midst
of their crosses, if they are faithful.

FRANÇOIS FÉNELON

Our God is so wonderfully good, and lovely,
and blessed in every way that the mere fact
of belonging to Him is enough for
an untellable fullness of joy!

HANNAH WHITALL SMITH

*Whom have I in heaven but You? And there
is none upon earth that I desire besides You.*

PSALM 73:25 NKJV

I Better Thing

If God, like a father, denies us what we want now,
it is in order to give us some far better thing later on.
The will of God, we can rest assured,
is invariably a better thing.

ELISABETH ELLIOT

God's kingdom isn't a matter of what you
put in your stomach, for goodness' sake.
It's what God does with your life as he sets it right,
puts it together, and completes it with joy.

ROMANS 14:17 MSG

The Creator thinks enough of you
to have sent Someone very special
so that you might have life—
abundantly, joyfully,
completely, and victoriously.

Give your heart's best treasure,
And the more you spend
From your little store,
With a double bounty,
God will give you more.

ADELAIDE ANN PROCTER

The God of the universe—the One who
created everything and holds it all in His hands—
created each of us in His image, to bear His likeness,
His imprint. It is only when Christ dwells within
our hearts, radiating the pure light of His love
through our humanity that we discover who we are
and what we were intended to be. There is no other
joy that reaches as deep or as wide or as high—
there is no other joy that is more complete.

WENDY MOORE

*Love is a circle...the more you give,
the more comes around.*

Enduring Faith

I abide in Christ and in doing so I find rest,
and the peace of God which passes all
understanding fills my heart and life.

JOHN HUNTER

Remain in me, and I will remain in you.
For a branch cannot produce fruit
if it is severed from the vine, and you
cannot be fruitful unless you remain in me.

JOHN 15:4 NLT

His justice is full and complete,
His mercy to us has no end;
the clouds are a path for His feet,
He comes on the wings of the wind.

CHRISTOPHER IDLE

Faith is what makes life bearable,
with all its tragedies and ambiguities
and sudden, startling joys.

MADELEINE L'ENGLE

A pure spirit is a sparkling stream,
full of clear thought, and continually
renewed in the crystal river of God's love.

JANET L. WEAVER SMITH

If one is joyful, it means that one is faithfully
living for God, and that nothing else counts; and
if one gives joy to others one is doing God's work.
With joy without and joy within, all is well.

JANET ERSKINE STUART

*You have granted me life and loving kindness;
and Your care has preserved my spirit.*

JOB 10:12 NASB

The Eyes of My Heart

Faith is the ability to let your light shine
even after your fuse is blown.
Faith is seeing light with the eyes of your heart,
when the eyes of your body see only darkness ahead.

BARBARA JOHNSON

If you have never heard the mountains singing,
or seen the trees of the field clapping their hands,
do not think because of that they don't.
Ask God to open your ears so you may hear it,
and your eyes so you may see it, because,
though few people ever know it,
they do, my friend, they do.

MCCANDLISH PHILLIPS

Open my eyes so I can see
what you show me of your miracle-wonders.

PSALM 119:18 MSG

Half the joy of life is in little things taken on the run.
Let us run if we must—even the sands do that—
but let us keep our hearts young and our eyes open
that nothing worth our while shall escape us.
And everything is worth its while
if we only grasp it and its significance.

VICTOR CHERBULIEZ

Open my eyes that I may see
Glimpses of truth Thou hast for me.
Place in my hands the wonderful key
That shall unclasp and set me free.

CLARA H. SCOTT

*It is only with the heart that one can see rightly.
What is essential is invisible to the eye.*

ANTOINE DE SAINT-EXUPÉRY

Nothing Is Impossible

Faith is the first factor in a life devoted to service.
Without faith, nothing is possible.
With it, nothing is impossible.

MARY McLEOD BETHUNE

Christian hope, unlike most other kinds of hope,
is not mere optimism. It's not even a matter of
thinking positively: "Cheer up. Things will
work out." Christian hope is applied faith.
If God Himself is here with us in His Holy Spirit,
then all things are possible.

BRUCE LARSON

Only those who see the invisible
can do the impossible.

Know therefore that the Lord your God is God,
the faithful God who maintains covenant loyalty
with those who love him and keep
his commandments, to a thousand generations.

DEUTERONOMY 7:9 NRSV

If we will make use of prayer to call down upon
ourselves and others those things which will glorify
the name of God, then...we shall see such answers
to prayer as we had never thought were possible.

OLE HALLESBY

If our faith is to have a firm foundation we must
be convinced beyond any possible doubt that
God is altogether worthy of our trust.

A. W. TOZER

The mind determines what's possible.
The soul surpasses it.

PILAR COOLINTA

Your steadfast love, O Lord,
extends to the heavens,
your faithfulness to the clouds.

PSALM 36:5 NRSV

Firm Foundation

God, your Father, is greater than your problems.
He can solve them all. Put your trust in
Him and you will experience this.

BASILEA SCHLINK

How firm a foundation, ye saints of the Lord,
Is laid for your faith in His excellent Word!
What more can He say than to you He hath said,
You, who unto Jesus for refuge have fled?...
Fear not, I am with thee, O be not dismayed,
For I am thy God and will still give thee aid;
I'll strengthen and help thee, and cause thee to stand
Upheld by My righteous, omnipotent hand.

R. KEEN

God's truth stands firm like a
foundation stone with this inscription:
"The Lord knows those who are his."

2 TIMOTHY 2:19 NLT

Faith in God is not blind. It is based on
His character and His promises.

Infinite and yet personal, personal and yet infinite,
God may be trusted because He is the True One.
He is true, He acts truly, and He speaks truly....
God's truthfulness is therefore foundational
for His trustworthiness.

Os Guinness

*Confidence is not based on wishful thinking,
but in knowing that God is in control.*

Everything in the heavens and on earth
is yours, O LORD.... Power and might
are in your hand, and at your discretion
people are made great and given strength.

1 Chronicles 29:11–12 nlt

The Gift of Faith

Lord...give me the gift of faith....
Teach me to live this moment only,
looking neither to the past with regret,
nor the future with apprehension.
Let love be my aim and my life a prayer.

ROSEANN ALEXANDER-ISHAM

God will do this, for he is faithful to do
what he says, and he has invited you into
partnership with his Son, Jesus Christ our Lord.

1 CORINTHIANS 1:9 NLT

Faith is given a glimpse of *something*,
however dimly. Men and women of faith know
they are strangers and exiles on the earth
because somehow and somewhere along the line
they have been given a glimpse of home.

FREDERICK BUECHNER

When faith is strong, troubles become trifles.
There can be comfort in sorrow because
in the midst of mourning, God gives a song.

BILLY GRAHAM

I took an inventory and looked into my little bag
to see what I had left over. I had one jewel
left in the bag, the brightest jewel of all.
I had the gift of faith.

LOLA FALANA

Trust in your Redeemer's strength...exercise what
faith you have, and by and by He shall rise
upon you with healing beneath His wings.
Go from faith to faith and you shall
receive blessing upon blessing.

CHARLES H. SPURGEON

*We have been greatly encouraged...because
you have remained strong in your faith.*

1 THESSALONIANS 3:7 NLT

A Certain Hope

Hope is definitely not the same thing as optimism.
It is not the conviction that something will
turn out well, but the certainty that something
makes sense, regardless of how it turns out.

VÁCLAV HAVEL

I never spoke with God
nor visited in Heaven,
Yet certain am I of the spot
as if the chart were given.

EMILY DICKINSON

There will always be the unknown.
There will always be the unprovable.
But faith confronts those frontiers
with a thrilling leap. Then life becomes
vibrant with adventure!

ROBERT SCHULLER

God guides us, despite our uncertainties and our
vagueness, even through our failings and mistakes....
He leads us step by step, from event to event.
Only afterwards, as we look back over the way we
have come and reconsider certain important
moments in our lives in the light of all that has
followed them, or when we survey the whole
progress of our lives, do we experience the feeling
of having been led without knowing it,
the feeling that God has mysteriously guided us.

PAUL TOURNIER

*Faith is the assurance of things hoped for,
the conviction of things not seen.*

HEBREWS 11:1 NRSV

Faith is a living, daring confidence in
God's grace, so sure and certain that a man
could stake his life on it a thousand times.

MARTIN LUTHER

Dare to Believe

Love is there for us, love so great that it does
not turn its face away from us. That Love is Jesus.
We can dare to hope and believe again.

GLORIA GAITHER

Whatever your years, there is
in every being's heart the love of wonder,
the undaunted challenges of events,
the unfailing childlike appetite for what
comes next, and the joy of the game of life.
You are as young as your hope.

DOUGLAS MACARTHUR

You are never alone. In your heart of hearts,
in the place where no two people are ever alike,
Christ is waiting for you. And what you
never dared hope for springs to life.

BROTHER ROGER OF TAIZÉ

At the very heart and foundation of all
God's dealings with us, however…mysterious
they may be, we must dare to believe in
and assert the infinite, unmerited,
and unchanging love of God.

L. B. COWMAN

Love makes burdens lighter, because you
divide them. It makes joys more intense,
because you share them. It makes you stronger,
so that you can reach out and become involved
with life in ways you dared not risk alone.

Therefore, since we have a great high priest
who has gone through the heavens,
Jesus the Son of God, let us hold
firmly to the faith we profess.

HEBREWS 4:14 NIV

*Faith in God gives your life a center from which
you can reach out and dare to love the world.*

BARBARA FARMER

In God We Trust

With God our trust can be...utterly free.
In Him are no limitations, no flaws, no weaknesses.
His judgment is perfect, His knowledge of us is
perfect, His love is perfect. God alone is trustworthy.

EUGENIA PRICE

Love GOD, your God. Walk in his ways.
Keep his commandments, regulations, and
rules so that you will live, really live,
live exuberantly, blessed by God.

DEUTERONOMY 30:16 MSG

It is only a tiny rosebud—
A flower of God's design;
But I cannot unfold the petals
With these clumsy hands of mine.

For the pathway that lies before me
My Heavenly Father knows—
I'll trust Him to unfold the moments
Just as He unfolds the rose.

God's timing is rarely our timing.
But far better than we do,
He numbers our days and knows
our moments and our hours.
Our task is to trust.

OS GUINNESS

The highest pinnacle of the spiritual life is not
joy in unbroken sunshine, but absolute and
undoubting trust in the love of God.

A. W. THOROLD

So faith bounds forward to its goal in God,
and love can trust her Lord to lead her there;
upheld by Him my soul is following hard,
till God hath full fulfilled my deepest prayer.

FREDERICK BROOK

*Trust involves letting go
and knowing God will catch you.*

JAMES DOBSON

Always Near

Lord, grant me a quiet mind, that trusting Thee,
for Thou art kind, I may go on without a fear,
for Thou, my Lord, art always near.

Amy Carmichael

It is good for me to draw near to God;
I have put my trust in the Lord GOD.

Psalm 73:28 NKJV

God still draws near to us in the ordinary,
commonplace, everyday experiences and places....
He comes in surprising ways.

Henry Gariepy

We need never shout across the spaces to an
absent God. He is nearer than our own soul,
closer than our most secret thoughts.

A. W. Tozer

We do not need to search for heaven,
over here or over there, in order to find
our eternal Father. In fact, we do not even
need to speak out loud, for though we speak in
the smallest whisper or the most fleeting thought,
He is close enough to hear us.

TERESA OF AVILA

*Draw near to God and
He will draw near to you.*

JAMES 4:8 NKJV

By putting the gift of yearning for God
into every human being's heart,
God at the same time draws all people
made in God's image to God's self
and into their own true selves.

ROBERTA BONDI

Faith Is Knowing

From the tiny birds of the air and from the
fragile lilies of the field we learn the same truth,
which is so important for those who desire
a life of simple faith: God takes care of His own.
He knows our needs. He anticipates our crises.
He is moved by our weaknesses. He stands
ready to come to our rescue. And at just the right
moment He steps in and proves Himself
as our faithful heavenly Father.

CHARLES SWINDOLL

Know by the light of faith that God is present,
and be content with directing all
your actions toward Him.

BROTHER LAWRENCE

*Faith is not believing that God can—
it's knowing that He will.*

Behold, I am with you and will keep you
wherever you go, and will bring you back
to this land; for I will not leave you
until I have done what I have promised you.

GENESIS 28:15 NASB

Faithful servants have a way of knowing
answered prayer when they see it, and
a way of not giving up when they don't.

MAX LUCADO

Living a life of faith means never knowing
where you are being led. But it does mean
loving and knowing the One who is leading.
It is literally a life of faith, not of
understanding and reason—a life of
knowing Him who calls us to go.

OSWALD CHAMBERS

Complete Trust

God does not allow us to continue to reduce
Him to a size and a shape we can manage.
He moves in our lives in ways that burst our
categories and overwhelm our finiteness.
When we realize He's bigger than
anything we can get our minds around,
we can begin to relax and enjoy Him.

PAULA RHINEHART

God wants us to feel that our way through life
is rough and perplexing, so that we may learn
thankfully to lean on Him. Therefore
He takes steps to drive us out of
self-confidence to trust in Himself—
for the secret of the godly life
is to "wait on the Lord."

J. I. PACKER

There is no unbelief;
Whoever plants a seed beneath the sod
And waits to see it push away the clod,
He trusts in God.

ELIZABETH YORK CASE

If you see that the job is too big for you, that it's
something only God can do, and you trust him
to do it...that trusting-him-to-do-it is what
gets you set right with God, by God.

ROMANS 4:4 MSG

God is looking for people who will come
in simple dependence upon His grace,
and rest in simple faith upon His greatness.
At this very moment, He's looking at you.

JACK HAYFORD

*The more we depend on God
the more dependable we find He is.*

CLIFF RICHARD

Faith Lights the Way

Faith, the spiritual strong searchlight,
illuminates the way, and although sinister doubts
may lurk…, I walk unafraid toward the
Enchanted Wood where…life and death are one
in the Presence of the Lord.

HELEN KELLER

Even though I walk through the darkest valley,
I fear no evil, for you are with me;
your rod and your staff—they comfort me.

PSALM 23:4 NRSV

It doesn't take a huge spotlight to draw attention
to how great our God is. All it takes is for one
committed person to so let their light shine before men,
that a world lost in darkness welcomes the light.

GARY SMALLEY AND JOHN TRENT

Let your faith in Christ, the omnipresent One,
be in the quiet confidence that He will every day
and every moment keep you as the apple of
His eye, keep you in perfect peace and in the
sure experience of all the light and the
strength you need in His service.

ANDREW MURRAY

Nothing can compare to the beauty and
greatness of the soul in which our King dwells
in His full majesty. No earthly fire can compare
with the light of its blazing love. No bastions
can compare with its ability to endure forever.

TERESA OF AVILA

*The shadows are behind you
if you walk toward the light.*

Time with Him

God loves to look at us, and loves it when we
will look back at Him. Even when we try to
run away from our troubles...God will find us,
bless us, even when we feel most alone, unsure....
God will find a way to let us know that
He is with us *in this place*, wherever we are.

KATHLEEN NORRIS

Open wide the windows of our spirits and fill us
full of light; open wide the door of our hearts
that we may receive and entertain You
with all the powers of our adoration.

CHRISTINA ROSSETTI

That is God's call to us—simply to be
people who are content to live close to Him
and to renew the kind of life in which the
closeness is felt and experienced.

THOMAS MERTON

There is a difference between living in Christ
and living for Christ.... He is more interested in
the time you spend with Him than with the
works you accomplish in His name.

CAROLYN LUNN

*Live carefree before God;
he is most careful with you.*

1 PETER 5:7 MSG

We need quiet time to examine our lives openly and
honestly.... Spending quiet time alone gives your
mind
an opportunity to renew itself and create order.

SUSAN L. TAYLOR

I will give thanks, O LORD, with all my heart...
As soon as I pray, you answer me;
you encourage me by giving me strength.

PSALM 138:1, 3 NLT

A Living Faith

Finding acceptance with joy, whatever the
circumstances of life—whether they are
petty annoyances or fiery trials—
this is a living faith that grows.

MARY LOU STEIGLEDER

By grace we see what we see.
To have faith is to respond to what we see
by longing for it the rest of our days;
by trying to live up to it and toward it
through all the wonderful and terrible things;
by breathing it in like air and growing strong on it;
by looking to see it again and see it better.

FREDERICK BUECHNER

Be patient with yourself and others.
There are no shortcuts to spirituality.
Growing fruit takes time.

Don't lose a minute in building on what you've
been given, complementing your basic faith with
good character, spiritual understanding...and generous
love, each dimension fitting into and developing
the others. With these qualities active and growing
in your lives...no day will pass without its reward as
you mature in your experience of our Master Jesus.

2 PETER 1:5–8 MSG

In a special way, human beings...being made in
the image of God, only become real human beings,
are only able to grow and thrive as human beings
as they also yearn for God.

ROBERTA BONDI

*I want to help you to grow as beautiful as God
meant you to be when He thought of you first.*

GEORGE MACDONALD

Our Refuge

To build in darkness does require faith.
But one day the light returns and you discover
that you have become a fortress...;
you may even find yourself...sought by others
as a beacon in their dark.

OLGA ROSMANITH

Call upon Me in the day of trouble;
I shall rescue you, and you will honor Me.

PSALM 50:15 NASB

When God has become our shepherd,
our refuge, our fortress, then we can reach out
to Him in the midst of a broken world and
feel at home while still on the way.

HENRI J. M. NOUWEN

God is our merciful Father and the source
of all comfort. He comforts us in all our troubles
so that we can comfort others. When they are
troubled, we will be able to give them
the same comfort God has given us.

When you accept the fact that sometimes seasons
are dry and times are hard and that God is in control
of both, you will discover a sense of divine refuge,
because the hope then is in God and not in yourself.

CHARLES SWINDOLL

*Let my soul take refuge...beneath the shadow
of Your wings: let my heart, this sea of
restless waves, find peace in You, O God.*

AUGUSTINE

God's Abundance

I think what we're longing for is not "the good life"
as it's been advertised to us in the American dream,
but life in its fullness, its richness, its abundance.
Living more reflectively helps us
enter into that fullness.

KEN GIRE

God is a rich and bountiful Father,
and He does not forget His children,
nor withhold from them anything which
it would be to their advantage to receive.

J. K. MACLEAN

He shall be like a tree planted by the rivers
of water, that brings forth its fruit in its season,
whose leaf also shall not wither;
and whatever he does shall prosper.

PSALM 1:3 NKJV

Faith is the bucket of power lowered by the
rope of prayer into the well of God's abundance.
What we bring up depends upon what we let down.
We have every encouragement to use a big bucket.

VIRGINIA WHITMAN

The grace of our Lord was exceedingly abundant,
with faith and love which are in Christ Jesus.

1 TIMOTHY 1:14 NKJV

*His overflowing love delights to make us
partakers of the bounties He graciously imparts.*

HANNAH MORE

The resource from which [God] gives is
boundless, measureless, unlimited, unending,
abundant, almighty, and eternal.

JACK HAYFORD

Trust in His Leading

You can trust the Lord too little,
but you can never trust Him too much.

My flesh and my heart fail;
but God is the strength of my heart
and my portion forever.

PSALM 73:26 NKJV

I always told Him, "I trust You.
I don't know where to go or what to do,
but I expect You to lead me," and He always did.

HARRIET TUBMAN

Trust! The way will open, the right issue will come,
the end will be peace, the cloud will be lifted,
and the light of eternal noonday shall shine at last.

L. B. COWMAN

In your unfailing love
you will lead the people you have redeemed.
In your strength you will guide them
to your holy dwelling.

EXODUS 15:13 NIV

The most effective...way to show
our love for God is to trust Him.

EUGENIA PRICE

When we trust, the Lord works.
What is done is not done by us, but by Him.

HANNAH WHITALL SMITH

Through Christ you have come to trust in God.
And you have placed your faith and hope
in God because he raised Christ from the dead
and gave him great glory.

1 PETER 1:21 NLT

Wait on the Lord

So wait before the Lord. Wait in the stillness.
And in that stillness, assurance will come to you.
You will know that you are heard;
you will know that your Lord ponders
the voice of your humble desires; you will
hear quiet words spoken to you yourself,
perhaps to your grateful surprise and refreshment.

AMY CARMICHAEL

The LORD longs to be gracious to you;
he rises to show you compassion.
For the LORD is a God of justice.
Blessed are all who wait for him!

ISAIAH 30:18 NIV

The way may at times seem dark, but light will arise,
if you trust in the Lord, and wait patiently for Him.

ELIZABETH T. KING

Lead me in Your truth and teach me,
For You are the God of my salvation;
On You I wait all the day.

*God makes a promise— faith believes it,
hope anticipates it, patience quietly awaits it.*

In all ranks of life the human heart yearns
for the beautiful; and the beautiful things
that God makes are His gift to all alike.

HARRIET BEECHER STOWE

Day by day the LORD takes care
of the innocent, and they will receive
an inheritance that lasts forever.

PSALM 37:18 NLT

Sustaining Faith

Faith...has sustained me—faith in the God
of the Bible, a God, as someone once put it,
not small enough to be understood
but big enough to be worshipped.

ELISABETH ELLIOT

For the eyes of the LORD run
to and fro throughout the whole earth,
to show Himself strong on behalf
of those whose heart is loyal to Him.

2 CHRONICLES 16:9 NKJV

We walk without fear, full of hope and courage
and strength to do His will, waiting for the
endless good which He is always giving
as fast as He can get us able to take it in.

GEORGE MACDONALD

God speaks to the crowd, but His call comes to
individuals, and through their personal obedience
He acts. He does not promise them nothing but success,
or even final victory in this life.... God does not
promise that He will protect them from trials,
from material cares, from sickness, from physical or
moral suffering. He promises only that He will be
with them in all these trials, and that He will
sustain them if they remain faithful to Him.

PAUL TOURNIER

Whate'er the care which breaks thy rest,
Whate'er the wish that swells thy breast;
Spread before God that wish, that care,
And change anxiety to prayer.

There is hope in your future, says the LORD.

JEREMIAH 31:17 NKJV

Eternally His

Day-to-day living becomes a window
through which we get a glimpse of life eternal.
The eternal illuminates and gives focus to the daily.

JANICE RIGGLE HUIE

Jesus, our Savior. He broke the power of death
and illuminated the way to life and
immortality through the Good News.

2 TIMOTHY 1:10 NLT

I believe in the immortality of the soul
because I have within me immortal longings.

HELEN KELLER

We are ever so secure
in the everlasting arms.

Heaven will be the endless portion
of those who have heaven in their soul.

Nothing we can do will make the Father love us less;
nothing we do can make Him love us more.
He loves us unconditionally with an everlasting love.
All He asks of us is that we respond to Him
with the free will that He has given to us.

NANCIE CARMICHAEL

As we follow Him who is everlasting
we will touch the things that last forever.

God's love is like a river springing up in the
Divine Substance and flowing endlessly through
His creation, filling all things with life
and goodness and strength.

THOMAS MERTON

I am wholly His; I am peculiarly His;
I am universally His; I am eternally His.

THOMAS BENTON BROOKS

Faith in Small Things

Faith in small things has repercussions
that ripple all the way out. In a huge, dark room
a little match can light up the place.

JONI EARECKSON TADA

If you have faith the size of a mustard seed,
you will say to this mountain, "Move from
here to there," and it will move;
and nothing will be impossible for you.

MATTHEW 17:20 NRSV

I am beginning to learn that it is the sweet, simple
things of life which are the real ones after all.

LAURA INGALLS WILDER

Just as angels are attracted to the light
of joy and kindness, so too are miracles
attracted to the lamp of faith and love.

MARY AUGUSTINE

Be faithful in little things, for in them
our strength lies. To the good God nothing is little,
because He is so great and we so small.

MOTHER TERESA

Is it so small a thing to have enjoyed the sun,
to have lived light in the spring, to have loved,
to have thought, to have done?

MATTHEW ARNOLD

Faith sees the invisible,
believes the incredible,
and receives the impossible.

*A little thing is a little thing, but
faithfulness in a little thing is a big thing.*

HUDSON TAYLOR

God Is in Control

What matters supremely is not the fact
that I know God, but the larger fact which
underlies it—the fact that He knows me.
I am graven on the palms of His hands.
I am never out of His mind. All my knowledge
of Him depends on His sustained initiative
in knowing me. I know Him because
He first knew me, and continues to know me.

J. I. PACKER

Confidence is not rooted in circumstances;
it is knowing that our times are in His hands.

Certainly God has heard; He has
given heed to the voice of my prayer.

PSALM 66:19 NASB

It's usually through our hard times, the unexpected
and not-according-to-plan times, that we experience
God in more intimate ways. We discover an
unquenchable longing to know Him more.
It's a passion that isn't concerned that life fall
within certain predictable lines, but a passion that
pursues God and knows He is relentless
in His pursuit of each one of us.

WENDY MOORE

*God gives the very best to those
who leave the choice to Him.*

"If you'll hold on to me for dear life,"
says GOD, "...I'll give you the best of care
if you'll only get to know and trust me."

PSALM 91:14–16 MSG

Rest in His Strength

Trust is giving up what little I have
in strength and power so I can confidently
relax in His power and strength.

GLORIA GAITHER

The LORD is my strength and my shield;
my heart trusts in him, and I am helped.
My heart leaps for joy and
I will give thanks to him in song.

PSALM 28:7 NIV

When God finds a soul that rests in Him and
is not easily moved, He operates within it in His
own manner. That soul allows God to do great
things within it. He gives to such a soul the key to
the treasures He has prepared for it so that it might
enjoy them. And to this same soul He gives the joy
of His presence which entirely absorbs such a soul.

CATHERINE OF GENOA

God does many things which we do not
understand.... A true faith must rest solidly
on [God's] character and His Word, not on our
particular conceptions of what He ought to do.

ELISABETH ELLIOT

In those times I can't seem to find God,
I rest in the assurance He knows how to find me.

NEVA COYLE

Strength, rest, guidance, grace, help,
sympathy, love—all from God to us!
What a list of blessings!

EVELYN STENBOCK

*God's peace is joy resting.
His joy is peace dancing.*

F. F. BRUCE

A Faithful Heart

Not everyone possesses...a conspicuous talent.
We are not equally blessed with great intellect
or physical beauty or emotional strength. But we
have all been given the same ability to be faithful.

GIGI GRAHAM TCHIVIDJIAN

Well done, my good and faithful servant.
You have been faithful in handling this
small amount, so now I will give you many
more responsibilities. Let's celebrate together!

MATTHEW 25:21 NLT

The greatest ability is dependability.

VANCE HAVNER

The important thing really is not the deed well done
or the medal that you possess, but the dedication
and dreams out of which they grow.

ROBERT H. BENSON

One hundred years from today your present
income will be inconsequential. One hundred years
from now it won't matter if you got that big break,
took the trip to Europe, or finally traded up to
a Mercedes.... It will matter that you knew God.
It will greatly matter, one hundred years from now,
that you made a commitment to Jesus Christ.

DAVID SHIBLEY

When you are inspired by a dream,
God has hit the ball into your court.
Now you have to hit it back with commitment.

ROBERT SCHULLER

Commit to hope. There's reason to!
For the believer, hope is divinely assured things
that aren't here yet! Our hope is grounded
in unshakable promises.

JACK HAYFORD

The Unknown Curve

The simple fact of being...in the presence of
the Lord and of showing Him all that I think,
feel, sense, and experience, without trying to hide
anything, must please Him. Somehow, somewhere,
I know that He loves me, even though I do not
feel that love as I can feel a human embrace,
even though I do not hear a voice as I hear
human words of consolation.... God is greater than
my senses, greater than my thoughts, greater than
my heart. I do believe that He touches me
in places that are unknown even to myself.

HENRI J. M. NOUWEN

Faith and doubt: both are needed—
not as antagonists, but working side by side—
to take us around the unknown curve.

LILLIAN SMITH

Faith brings us on highways
that make our reasoning dizzy.

CORRIE TEN BOOM

The unknown is not so frightening when
we realize that our all-knowing God is in it.

STORMIE OMARTIAN

I proclaim to you new things from this time,
Even hidden things which you have not known.

ISAIAH 48:6 NASB

I know that God is faithful.
I know that He answers prayers,
many times in ways I may not understand.

SHEILA WALSH

If anyone loves God, he is known by Him.

1 CORINTHIANS 8:3 NASB

Draw Near to God

Whoso draws nigh to God,
one step through doubtings dim,
God will advance a mile
in blazing light to him.

We are of such value to God that He came
to live among us...and to guide us home.
He will go to any length to seek us, even to
being lifted high upon the cross to draw us
back to Himself. We can only respond
by loving God for His love.

CATHERINE OF SIENNA

God proves to be good to
the man who passionately waits,
to the woman who diligently seeks.
It's a good thing to quietly hope,
quietly hope for help from God.

LAMENTATIONS 3:25–26 MSG

A living, loving God can and does make
His presence felt, can and does speak to us
in the silence of our hearts, can and does
warm and caress us till we no longer doubt
that He is near, that He is here.

BRENNAN MANNING

I have sought Thy nearness;
With all my heart have I called Thee,
And going out to meet Thee
I found Thee coming toward me.

YEHUDA HALEVI

*Let us draw near to God.... Let us hold
unswervingly to the hope we profess,
for he who promised is faithful.*

HEBREWS 10:22–23 NIV

Walk of Faith

My Lord God, I have no idea where
I am going. I do not see the road ahead
of me. I cannot know for certain where
it will end.... But I believe that the desire
to please You does in fact please You.
And I hope I have that desire in all that
I am doing. I hope that I will never do
anything apart from that desire.
And I know that if I do this, You will
lead me by the right road though
I may know nothing about it.

Therefore will I trust You always
though I may seem to be lost and
in the shadow of death. I will not fear,
for You are ever with me.
And You will never leave me
to face my perils alone.

THOMAS MERTON

Forbid that I should walk through
Thy beautiful world with unseeing eyes:
Forbid that the lure of the market-place
should ever entirely steal my heart away from
the love of the open acres and the green trees:
Forbid that under the low roof of workshop
or office or study I should ever forget
Thy great overarching sky.

JOHN BAILLIE

*Yet I am always with you;
you hold me by my right hand.*

PSALM 73:23 NIV

I will look with favor on the faithful in the land,
so that they may live with me; whoever walks
in the way that is blameless shall minister to me.

PSALM 101:6 NRSV

In His Light

Sunshine spills through autumn-colored leaves,
lighting up their brilliance like stained-glass
windows in a great cathedral, expressing the
wonder of God's love, declaring His glory.

Turn your eyes upon Jesus,
look full in His wonderful face,
and the things of earth will grow strangely dim,
by the light of His glory and grace.

HELEN LIMMEL

Let us fix our eyes on Jesus, the author and
perfecter of our faith, who for the joy set
before him endured the cross,…and sat down
at the right hand of the throne of God.

HEBREWS 12:2 NIV

From the world we see, hear, and touch, we behold
inspired visions that reveal God's glory. In the
sun's light, we catch warm rays of grace and glimpse
His eternal design. In the birds' song, we hear
His voice and it reawakens our need of Him.
At the wind's touch, we feel His Spirit
and sense our eternal existence.

WENDY MOORE

You have set Your glory above the heavens.
Thy glory flames from sun and star:
Center and soul of every sphere,
Yet to each loving heart how near.

OLIVER WENDELL HOLMES

*Our fulfillment comes in knowing God's glory,
loving Him for it, and rejoicing in it.*

ROBERT COLEMAN

Believing Is Seeing

By faith, we see the world called into
existence by God's word, what we see
created by what we don't see.

HEBREWS 11:3 MSG

I would rather live in a world where my life
is surrounded by mystery than live in a world
so small that my mind could comprehend it.

HARRY EMERSON FOSDICK

I am still confident of this:
I will see the goodness of the LORD
in the land of the living.
Wait for the LORD;
be strong and take heart
and wait for the LORD.

PSALM 27:13–14 NIV

Open your mouth and taste, open your
eyes and see—how good GOD is.
Blessed are you who run to him.
Worship GOD if you want the best;
worship opens doors to all his goodness.

PSALM 34:8–9 MSG

When faithfulness is most difficult,
it can be most rewarding.

If we are children of God, we have a
tremendous treasure in nature and will realize
that it is holy and sacred. We will see God
reaching out to us in every wind that blows,
every sunrise and sunset, every cloud in the sky,
every flower that blooms, and every leaf that fades.

OSWALD CHAMBERS

Some things have to be believed to be seen.

LYNN YEAKEL

Blessings from Above

Lift up your eyes. Your heavenly Father
waits to bless you—in inconceivable ways to make
your life what you never dreamed it could be.

ANNE ORTLUND

O Lord, you are a great and awesome God!
You always fulfill your covenant and
keep your promises of unfailing love to those
who love you and obey your commands.

DANIEL 9:4 NLT

I wish you love, and strength, and faith, and wisdom,
Goods, gold enough to help some needy one.
I wish you songs, but also blessed silence,
And God's sweet peace when every day is done.

DOROTHY NELL MCDONALD

The heavenly Father welcomes us with open arms
and imparts to us blessing upon blessing—
not because we are upright but because
Jesus Christ has clothed us with His own virtue.

God puts each fresh morning,
each new chance of life, into our hands
as a gift to see what we will do with it.

May the LORD, the God of your fathers, increase you
a thousand-fold more than you are and bless you,
just as He has promised you!

DEUTERONOMY 1:11 NASB

Be on the lookout for mercies. The more we
look for them, the more of them we will see.
Blessings brighten when we count them.

MALTBIE D. BABCOCK

Perfect Peace

Do not let your heart be troubled;
believe in God, believe also in Me.
In My Father's house are many dwelling places;
if it were not so, I would have told you;
for I go to prepare a place for you.
If I go and prepare a place for you,
I will come again and receive you to Myself,
that where I am, there you may be also....
I will not leave you as orphans;
I will come to you.... Peace I leave with you;
My peace I give to you; not as
the world gives do I give to you.
Do not let your heart be troubled,
nor let it be fearful.

JOHN 14:1–3, 18, 27 NASB

The God of peace gives perfect peace to those
whose hearts are stayed upon Him.

CHARLES H. SPURGEON

Joy is not happiness so much as gladness;
it is the ecstasy of eternity in a soul that has made
peace with God and is ready to do His will.

You will keep in perfect peace
him whose mind is steadfast,
because he trusts in you.

ISAIAH 26:3 NIV

Have courage for the great sorrows of life,
and patience for the small ones; and when
you have...accomplished your daily task,
go to sleep in peace. God is awake.

VICTOR HUGO

*Only God gives true peace—a quiet gift
He sets within us just when we think
we've exhausted our search for it.*

God's Power at Work

I pray that you, being rooted and
established in love, may have power,
together with all the saints, to grasp
how wide and long and high and
deep is the love of Christ, and to know
this love that surpasses knowledge—
that you may be filled to the measure of
all the fullness of God. Now to him who
is able to do immeasurably more than
all we ask or imagine, according to
his power that is at work within us,
to him be glory in the church and in
Christ Jesus throughout all generations,
for ever and ever! Amen.

EPHESIANS 3:17–21 NIV

*God has not given us a spirit of fear and timidity,
but of power, love, and self-discipline.*

2 TIMOTHY 1:7 NLT

God longs to give favor—that is,
spiritual strength and health—to those
who seek Him, and Him alone.
He grants spiritual favors and victories,
not because the one who seeks Him
is holier than anyone else, but in order to
make His holy beauty and His great
redeeming power known.... For it is through
the living witness of others that we are
drawn to God at all. It is because of His
creatures, and His work in them,
that we come to praise Him.

TERESA OF AVILA

The light of God surrounds me;
The love of God enfolds me;
The power of God protects me;
The presence of God watches over me.
Wherever I am, God is.

Enfolded in His Peace

Calm me, O Lord, as You stilled the storm,
Still me, O Lord, keep me from harm.
Let all the tumult within me cease,
Enfold me, Lord, in Your peace.

CELTIC TRADITIONAL

Don't fret or worry. Instead of
worrying, pray. Let petitions and praises
shape your worries into prayers,
letting God know your concerns.
Before you know it, a sense of
God's wholeness, everything coming
together for good, will come and
settle you down. It's wonderful
what happens when Christ displaces
worry at the center of your life.

PHILIPPIANS 4:6–7 MSG

Nothing in all creation
is so like God as stillness.

MEISTER ECKHART

O this full and perfect peace,
O this transport all divine—
In a love which cannot cease,
I am His, and He is mine.

GEORGE WADE ROBINSON

The peace of God is that eternal calm
which lies far too deep down to be reached
by any external trouble or disturbance.

A. T. PIERSON

If peace be in the heart
the wildest winter storm
is full of solemn beauty.

C. F. RICHARDSON

God cannot give us a happiness and peace
apart from Himself, because it is not there.
There is no such thing.

C. S. LEWIS

Renewing Promises

Each time a rainbow appears, stretching
from one end of the sky to the other,
it's God renewing His promise.
Each shade of color, each facet of light
displays the radiant spectrum of God's love—
a promise that life can be new for each one of us.

The joyful birds prolong the strain,
their song with every spring renewed;
the air we breathe, and falling rain,
each softly whispers: God is good.

JOHN HAMPDEN GURNEY

May God give you eyes to see beauty
only the heart can understand.

All the world is an utterance of the Almighty.
Its countless beauties, its exquisite adaptations,
all speak to you of Him.

PHILLIPS BROOKS

Not every day of our lives is overflowing
with joy and celebration. But there are moments
when our hearts nearly burst within us for the
sheer joy of being alive. The first sight of
our newborn babies, the warmth of love
in another's eyes, the fresh scent of rain
on a hot summer's eve—moments like these
renew in us a heartfelt appreciation for life.

GWEN ELLIS

*Oh, worship the LORD
in the beauty of holiness!*

PSALM 96:9 NKJV

Our Creator would never have made
such lovely days, and given us the deep hearts
to enjoy them, above and beyond all thought,
unless we were meant to be immortal.

NATHANIEL HAWTHORNE

Faithful in Prayer

Prayer is such an ordinary, everyday,
mundane thing. Certainly, people who pray
are no more saints than the rest of us.
Rather, they are people who want to share
a life with God, to love and be loved,
to speak and to listen, to work and to be
at rest in the presence of God.

ROBERTA BONDI

The privilege of prayer to me is one of
the most cherished possessions, because
faith and experience alike convince me
that God Himself sees and answers.

SIR WILFRED GRENFELL

Nothing in your daily life is so insignificant
and so inconsequential that God will not
help you by answering your prayer.

OLE HALLESBY

Sometimes remembering the day of our
salvation or remembering answered prayer
is the last knot on the end of our rope to cling to.
When we're struggling with doubts, looking back
at the foundation of our faith is a positive activity.

VIRGINIA THOMAS

*Prayer should be the key of the day
and the lock of the night.*

Can we find a friend so faithful,
Who will all our sorrows share?
Jesus knows our every weakness:
Take it to the Lord in prayer.

GEORGE SCRIVEN

Give your burdens to the LORD,
and he will take care of you.

PSALM 55:22 NLT

Leave It to God

Because God is responsible for our welfare,
we are told to cast all our care upon Him, for
He cares for us. God says, "I'll take the burden—
don't give it a thought—leave it to Me."
God is keenly aware that we are dependent
upon Him for life's necessities.

BILLY GRAHAM

Prayer...is bona fide letting go, but it is a release
with hope. We have no fatalist resignation. We are
buoyed up by a confident trust in the character of God.

RICHARD J. FOSTER

If you are at a place in your life where you
feel like you can't take one step without
the Lord's help, be glad.
He has you where He wants you.

STORMIE OMARTIAN

Contentment comes as the infallible result of
great acceptances, great humilities—of not
trying to make ourselves this or that, but
of surrendering ourselves to the fullness of life—
of letting life flow through us.

DAVID GRAYSON

*I pray hard, work hard,
and leave the rest to God.*

FLORENCE GRIFFITH JOYNER

Those who know Your name
will put their trust in You,
for You, O LORD, have not forsaken
those who seek You.

PSALM 9:10 NASB

*I believe the promises of God enough
to venture an eternity on them.*

G. CAMPBELL MORGAN